INSPIRING GENEROSITY

INSPIRING
GENEROSITY

BARBARA BONNER

WISDOM PUBLICATIONS • BOSTON

Wisdom Publications
199 Elm Street
Somerville, MA 02144 USA
www.wisdompubs.org

*Library of Congress Cataloging-in-Publication
Data*
Bonner, Barbara, 1948–
  Inspiring generosity / Barbara Bonner.
    pages cm
  Includes bibliographical references and index.
  ISBN-13: 978-1-61429-110-7 (pbk. : alk. paper)
  ISBN-10: 1-61429-110-1 (pbk. : alk. paper)
  ISBN-13: 978-1-61429-130-5 (eBook)
  1. Generosity. I. Title.
  BJ1533.G4B66 2014
  179'.9—dc23
                        2013026575

18 17 16 15 14
 6   5   4   3   2

Cover design by Phil Pascuzzo.
Interior design by Gopa&Ted2, Inc.
Set in ITC Galliard Pro 10.5/16.
Author photo by Nancy Crampton.

Wisdom Publications' books are printed on
acid-free paper and meet the guidelines for
permanence and durability of the Production
Guidelines for Book Longevity of the Council
on Library Resources.

This book was produced with environmental
mindfulness. For more information, please visit
our website, www.wisdompubs.org. This paper
is FSC® certified.

Printed in the United States of America.

Visit www.fscus.org.

EVEN AFTER ALL THIS TIME,

THE SUN NEVER SAYS TO THE EARTH,

"YOU OWE ME."

LOOK WHAT HAPPENS WITH

A LOVE LIKE THAT.

IT LIGHTS

THE WHOLE SKY. HAFIZ

Introduction

WHAT IS GENEROSITY?

GENEROSITY is an activity that can change the world. It works its magic on one person at a time; then, almost effortlessly, its beautiful multiplying force animates families, friends, communities, cultures, and the world at large.

Unlike its close cousin, compassion, generosity requires *action*. To be a generous person, you must act. In many ways, generosity is compassion in action, and it is love in action. It's no surprise that generosity is at the very heart of all the world's major religions.

Generosity is a practice. And as with anything we practice, we get better at it over time. It's a muscle that needs exercise. Generous actions have impact on the beneficiaries, but they also change the lives of the generous in remarkable ways. Generosity can transform our place in the world and how we live our lives. Generosity can be revolutionary.

Generosity is often confused with giving. There are many ways to give. We all have something to give—our time, our caring and caretaking, a kind word, a smile, encouragement, material gifts of all kinds. But all giving does not necessarily fit my definition of generosity. You can give with the expectation of receiving acclaim for your gift. You can give to create a certain outcome that will benefit you personally. You can give in order to be in the company of people who will be impressed by your ability to give. And you can give from a generous place in your heart that propels you forward to provide what is needed, with little concern for applause and recognition for yourself.

Generosity is often quite bold, ignoring the advice of friends and family and moving forward with courage and conviction. Generosity is willing to take risks. In fact, risks have little constraint on a generous heart.

Generosity invites us to put ourselves in another's shoes, see and feel the existence of a pressing need, realize that it is within our power to help, and then act in whatever way we can. It's really as simple as that.

THE INVITATION

This little book is an invitation to savor a sampling of the very best inspirations on the subject of generosity—leading voices from across cultures and centuries, wise words from the worlds of religion and spirituality, moving stories about contemporary people whose lives have been transformed by the power of generosity, and eloquent poems on the theme of generosity. I invite you to dip in and enjoy a few pages at a time—or curl up for an afternoon and read them all. You can start anywhere—this book has no beginning, middle, or end.

In bringing together these moments of generosity, I have had the great joy of spending three years immersed in the study of this magnificent quality in its many forms and flavors. After a professional lifetime working in philanthropy, I have become a student again in creating this book. I have studied how generosity has been regarded through the lenses of history and religion, as elucidated in the Bible, the Koran, the Torah, Buddhist texts, and the Tao Te Ching. I have worked with poets and literature professors to comb through the best poems of the last six centuries for those that have generosity at their heart. I have read hundreds of accounts of people whose lives were struck by what I call a "lightning bolt of generosity" that transformed their lives. I have studied the current scientific literature on whether humans are altruistic by nature (recent work points to *yes*), what chemical substances serve to make us more or less generous, and what areas of the brain light up when we are engaged in generous acts. I have attended conferences and retreats all over the world, most notably in Zurich for a remarkable meeting headed by the Dalai Lama, with economists, scientists, and Buddhist scholars who are exploring altruism in its many forms. (For those who want to dive more deeply into the literature of generosity, the book's website, www.inspiringgenerosity.net, includes a comprehensive reference bibliography of the main sources that guided me.)

I hope readers will want to give this book as a token of gratitude to all the generous people in their lives. I hope it will make its way to desks, coffee tables, and bedside tables, as well as beach chairs, pulpits, and meditation cushions. I hope that philanthropists and leaders of our foundations and charitable arms of our businesses will display this book in their homes and offices, turning to it to renew the spiritual engine of their work. Nonprofit boards and executives should have this book, and they should give it to those who donate to the organizations they lead. Fundraisers should have this book on their desks and make it a gift to the generous people who light up their work. Retreat centers will want to make this book available to their students, teachers, participants, and guests. Volunteers could be given this book as a token of appreciation for all they do—and perhaps many will have already bought it for themselves! Teachers, professors, religious leaders, poets, and philosophers will all find inspiration in these pages. I even dare hope that our elected officials, who could all do with a bit more generosity of spirit, may find this book a source of inspiration.

A BELL IS NO BELL TIL YOU RING IT

A SONG IS NO SONG TIL YOU SING IT

AND LOVE IN YOUR HEART WASN'T
PUT THERE TO STAY—

LOVE ISN'T LOVE TIL YOU GIVE IT AWAY.

OSCAR HAMMERSTEIN II

GENEROSITY AND PHILANTHROPY

There are as many forms of philanthropy as there are motives to give. American philanthropy is a uniquely wonderful phenomenon. Our museums, universities and colleges, opera houses and symphony orchestras, hospitals, libraries, and national parks owe their origins in large measure to the charitable giving of very wealthy philanthropists who have profited in extraordinary ways from success in American business. Some of these philanthropic gifts are meant to enhance our culture in ways the giver deemed important. Some are made to crown the givers in glory. Many philanthropists consider their giving akin to investing. Others give out of a spirit of enlightened generosity—a desire to give back to a world that has been immensely good to them. And the true angels step forward and ask: How can I help? How much do you need? How can we work together to change things?

We live in a culture in which philanthropy is everyday news. We are surrounded by an impressive army of philanthropic billionaires who put large chunks of their fortunes to work for the greater good. Successful, socially aware business leaders like Warren Buffett, Bill Gates, and George Soros have poured vast sums into nonprofit organizations designed to dramatically improve the quality of life of those in great need.

In times of catastrophe, Americans respond with remarkable charitable giving. In the days following the Asian tsunami of 2004, Hurricanes Sandy and Katrina, and the earthquake in Haiti, Americans opened their hearts and wallets with truly staggering generosity. I venture to say that, in each case, the individual act of giving, whether $5 or $5,000, gave the donor a deepened sense of meaning and participation in the stream of life that far surpassed the amount of the gift.

People pull together in their desire to help. We witnessed a dramatic moment of

KINDNESS IS THE PRACTICE OF GENEROSITY.

SHARON SALZBERG

coming together as a national and international community after the attacks of 9/11, when neighbor helped neighbor in profoundly selfless and generous ways. It is in our genetic makeup to help, to offer, to step forward to make a difference. Recent scientific research points convincingly to an inborn human altruism.

But while we are a generous nation, it is worth remembering that 97 million Americans live in poverty today. And when we look abroad, the numbers are more staggering. In our world of plenty, 10 million children under the age of five die every year from causes related to poverty—that's 27,000 every day. As our most noted contemporary American philanthropist, Bill Gates, says, "Is the rich world aware of how four billion of six billion live? If we were aware, we would want to help out, we'd want to get involved." I would add that the need might be in remote Africa or just down the block. We can all make a difference in so many different ways. As former President Bill Clinton, who has now devoted much of his life's work to philanthropy, says, "When we give what we can and give it with joy, we don't just renew the American tradition of giving, we also renew ourselves."

One of the great paradoxes of this time of increased philanthropy is that we are also the most self-involved, materialistic, grasping, distracted, ridiculously overconsuming culture in recent memory. Even the professions of philanthropy and fundraising often seem to have lost their way. Endlessly polishing their systems, policies, and procedures, they sometimes seem to forget that they provide the dynamic link between generous individuals and enormous needs. All too often, fundraising crosses the line into persuasion and arm-twisting to extract large gifts and meet ever-increasing institutional goals. We create relationships of exchange when we would be better served developing cultures of generosity.

UNLESS SOMEONE LIKE YOU CARES
A WHOLE AWFUL LOT,

NOTHING IS GOING TO GET BETTER.
IT'S NOT.

DR. SEUSS

MY PATH TO GENEROSITY

I grew up in a world of great economic privilege that felt nearly completely lacking in generosity. The 1960s in this country were times of very real need. But in Columbus, Ohio, I neither heard nor saw any of it. Neither did I know about the poverty of Appalachia or the civil rights marches in the South. Looking back, the well-off people in that little Midwestern world seemed by and large quite oblivious to a larger world of human need. I don't remember any of the adults in my world discussing philanthropy as it related to local or distant causes or social needs. My parents were kind, compassionate, well-educated, well-meaning people whom I dearly loved. But they had not been raised in families noted for their generosity. The "generosity gene" had apparently passed them by. For some reason that still remains mysterious to me, I was always distressed by this, even somewhat embarrassed.

For as long as I can remember, I have loved the ritual of gift giving, giving things away, and working toward opening up possibilities where none seemed to exist. In my career, I have always been drawn to philanthropists guided by extraordinarily generous hearts who have stepped forward in remarkable ways to make a difference in the world.

I started my professional life as an art historian, quickly moving into a career in museums as a curator, deputy director, and director. The artistic missions and the programs that supported them mattered deeply to me. But, increasingly, the relationships with generous champions who were galvanized by the museums' work were what both fascinated and fulfilled me. In leadership positions at Bennington College and later at Kripalu Center for Yoga & Health, what moved me most was helping to create cultures of generosity. Now, as a consultant to nonprofits, I have the luxury of working with those organizations whose missions wrap around my heart. Additionally, my service on

10 nonprofit boards and my role as cofounder of a charitable fund for women with cancer who are living in poverty have dramatically deepened my connections to multitudes of generous individuals who are eager to make a difference. While I don't pretend to be an expert in the field of generosity, I have certainly been an observer with a very good front-row seat.

In the final days of creating this book, I was in New York City for a day of meetings. On the subway downtown, a man who was clearly in serious need stepped into the car and asked everyone to listen to him. He told us that he was a military veteran who now lives in the New York City shelters. He has no money and is hungry. He implored my fellow passengers for help, adding, poignantly, "Don't be embarrassed to help me."

To my surprise, five or six people immediately reached for their wallets or purses. One woman gave him the full bag of groceries that she had just bought. The lessons of writing this book are in my bones now, so I did not hesitate for a moment as I reached into my purse to see what I could offer. It wasn't much. As I placed a modest handful of quarters in his bag, I told him I was sorry I couldn't do more.

He looked deep into my eyes with tremendous concentration and sweetness and said, "It is not how much you give me. It is that you opened your heart to me."

There it was. All the beautiful reading and research for a book on generosity now lived in the eyes and words of one man I will never forget.

THE "LIGHTNING-BOLT MOMENT"

Time after time, I hear that the desire to act generously has arrived in someone's life as an uninvited guest, unexpectedly, like a lightning bolt, in a mere moment. A gesture, a news story, a quotation in a book, a passing remark can change everything. For many, that moment is enough for generosity to move into their hearts and minds and become central to their lives. This book is my offering of such moments.

You will read about Sasha Dichter's train ride home from an ordinary workday and his encounter with a fellow passenger that changed his life. Betty Londergan went to the movies and emerged a philanthropist with a revolutionary daily practice. Rising-star chef Narayanan Krishnan stepped out of a hotel onto a street in India—and what he saw turned his life upside down and propelled him toward a calling of nearly unimaginable service. Fourteen such stories about what I call "generosity heroes," none of whom are famous and only one of whom is wealthy, invite you to become inspired.

You will read the classic poetry of Shakespeare, Hafiz, Emily Dickinson, and George Eliot, and the modern voices of Wendell Berry, Sharon Olds, A. R. Ammons, Naomi Shibab Nye, Donald Justice, and many others.

You will read flashes of insight into the heart of generosity from voices across centuries and continents: Winston Churchill, Mother Teresa, Maya Angelou, Gandhi, Dr. Martin Luther King Jr., John Steinbeck, James Joyce, Leo Tolstoy, Walt Whitman, Henry David Thoreau, Goethe, Seneca, Albert Schweitzer, and Anne Frank—to name only a few of more than a hundred collected here.

As you read, I invite you to open your heart to the power of your own innate generosity, your desire to make a difference in the world, to help make someone's day a little brighter or that person's world a bit more secure. Let the words wash over you, and savor the sensations that the memories, dreams, and aspirations evoke. My hope is that this book kindles a spark in your heart that moves you into the sunshine of a more generous life. And if your life is more generous, we all prosper.

That is one of generosity's most wonderful qualities: it is utterly contagious.

"Generosity is the most natural outward

expression of an inner attitude of compassion and loving-

kindness. When one desires to alleviate the suffering of others

and to promote their well-being, then generosity—in action,

word, and thought—is this desire put into practice. It is important

to recognize the 'generosity' here refers not just to giving in

a material sense, but to generosity of the heart."

THE DALAI LAMA

The Story of Sasha Dichter

THERE WAS NOTHING particularly different about that day. Sasha Dichter was on the S train as usual, heading home from his job in Manhattan as Chief Innovation Officer at the Acumen Fund. As often happens on the MTA, a beggar was asking for money, which he said would be used to purchase food and supplies for the homeless. And, also as usual, everyone was saying no, including Sasha.

But then, it happened: Sasha was struck by a generosity lightning bolt. In a flash, he realized he'd made the wrong choice. In that moment, something in his heart opened to the idea of doing things differently. "I wanted to stop saying no," he recalls. "I needed to break this habit. I decided I was hiding behind doing what is 'smart.'"

Sasha's professional world involves designing and financing massive projects to help people in the world's poorest areas. His work is at the intersection of philanthropy and business, in search of global solutions for some of our most intransigent problems related to poverty. And yet he had just discovered that he was not personally generous. The realization jolted him into a new awareness: "'No' can become who you are," he says. "I needed a new habit and a new reflex."

On the spot, he decided that for the next month he would answer only "yes" to any and all requests for money. Beggars, nonprofits, street musicians, mail solicitations— they would all get a "yes." It was December, so he got a lot of practice addressing the endless stream of year-end appeals in his mailbox. Friends warned Sasha to be cautious, to consider if giving to an organization might be wiser than giving money to a stranger who might use it on drugs or alcohol. But for this month, he resisted employing the careful scrutiny so essential to his professional life. "What was smart was keeping me from doing what was right," he says.

We can't always know or count on the results of our generosity. From his work, Sasha had learned that "the smartest philanthropists lead with generosity," and, in fact, philanthropy itself "is about risk-taking—risks that others won't take." Generosity also requires practice, he observed, as the month progressed—and he "started to feel like a generous person." We may have innate capacities for generosity, but they need to be exercised.

Sasha soon learned that his experiment was never really about donating money. What he was giving himself was "a chance to test what it felt like to live with a totally different orientation. It was a commitment to take a door that was too closed for my taste, and open it wide."

In my own work with generous people, Sasha's words are borne out over and over again. All of them have had a moment when they have decided to step into a more generous life. Then they have exercised that muscle in a repetitive practice, until the generous act becomes second nature. The effect of the exercise gives every appearance of an "unlocking" of an innate generosity that has been waiting to take shape.

Beyond the lessons of philanthropy, Sasha saw just how deeply "people are hungering for something more in their lives—more connection and more meaning." Generosity is a beautiful choice on that path.

Since that moment on the S train, Sasha has fully embraced his "new habit" of giving. His daily blog that started as a wonderful account of his month of giving now offers his ongoing reflections on generosity in its many manifestations in the larger world. His TED talk on the experiment is one of the most popular in the series. One of Sasha's recent projects has been a well-orchestrated media effort to transform Valentine's Day into "Generosity Day."

"Love the earth and sun and the animals,

despise riches, give alms to every one that asks, stand up

for the stupid and crazy, devote your income and your

labor for others . . . and your very flesh shall be a great poem

and have the richest fluency not only in its words but in the

silent lines of its lips and face and between the lashes

of your eyes and in every motion and joint of your body."

WALT WHITMAN

"When you are practicing generosity,

you should feel a little pinch when you give something

away. That pinch is your stinginess protesting. If you give away

your old, worn-out coat that you wouldn't be caught dead wearing,

that is not generosity. There is no pinch. You are doing nothing

to overcome your stinginess; you're just cleaning out your closet

and calling it something else. Giving away your coat might keep

someone warm, but it does not address the problem . . .

to free ourselves from self-cherishing and self-grasping."

GEHLEK RIMPOCHÉ

MY PIECE OF BREAD
ONLY BELONGS TO ME
WHEN I KNOW THAT
EVERYONE ELSE
HAS A SHARE, AND THAT
NO ONE STARVES
WHILE I EAT. LEO TOLSTOY

THE WISH TO BE GENEROUS

All that I serve will die, all my delights,
the flesh kindled from my flesh, garden and field,
the silent lilies standing in the woods,
the woods, the hill, the whole earth, all
will burn in man's evil, or dwindle
in its own age. Let the world bring on me
the sleep of darkness without stars, so I may know
my little light taken from me into the seed
of the beginning and the end, so I may bow
to mystery, and take my stand on the earth
like a tree in a field, passing without haste
or regret toward what will be, my life
a patient willing descent into the grass.

WENDELL BERRY

"If a beggar approaches me

and puts out his hand, and if I only have

a $10 bill, I have to give it to him. It's none

of my business whether he plans to spend it

on infant formula for his starving baby or

on a pint of Thunderbird."

BARBARA EHRENREICH

IF YOU CAN'T FEED A HUNDRED PEOPLE,

THEN JUST FEED ONE.

MOTHER TERESA

GIVE ALL THOU CANST; HIGH HEAVEN REJECTS THE LORE OF NICELY-CALCULATED LESS OR MORE.

WILLIAM WORDSWORTH

"To cultivate generosity directly

is another fundamental part of living a spiritual life.

Like the training precepts and like our inner meditations,

generosity can actually be practiced. With practice, its spirit

forms our actions, and our hearts will grow stronger and lighter.

It can lead to new levels of letting go and great happiness."

JACK KORNFIELD

"Jesus's standard of generosity

is not the world's standard. 'Just give a cup of

cold water in my name,' he instructs. So little

and so simple as to be scarcely noticed! Like the

widow's mite, it is nevertheless a high standard.

It demands that we live in awareness of the

thirst all around us."

MARGARET GUENTHER

"One practice of generosity

that I've found very helpful is that when

a thought to give arises, I try to act on it,

rather than second-guessing myself. I've never

regretted these moments of giving."

JOSEPH GOLDSTEIN

"BEGIN WHERE YOU ARE AND SUCH AS YOU ARE,
WITHOUT AIMING MAINLY TO BECOME OF MORE
WORTH, AND WITH KINDNESS AFORETHOUGHT
GO ABOUT DOING GOOD."

HENRY DAVID THOREAU

The Story of Mary Donnelly

ON BLOCK ISLAND, 13 miles off Rhode Island's mainland, Mary Donnelly, an 83-year-old mother of seven and grandmother of six, is something of a legend. The Mary D. Fund, which she established in 1979, has helped close to a third of islanders with basic needs like rent, medical bills, and mortgage payments.

The longest-working employee of the state of Rhode Island, Mary has been the public-health nurse on this doctorless island for 55 years. In a place where house calls are still a routine manner of health-care delivery, she attends to the medical needs of a year-round population of more than a thousand. Her job allows her to see close up the sometimes crippling financial needs of residents whose income drops off dramatically when the wealthy second-homeowners and vacationers depart after Labor Day. As unemployment can climb upward of 27 percent in the winter months, and essential fuel, medical, and electric bills go unpaid, many of Block Island's year-round residents have come to rely on the generosity of the Mary D. Fund.

Supported entirely by contributions from individuals who hear about her work, and by the annual Mary D. Ball in the summer, the Mary D. Fund gives away about $50,000 a year in small, individual gifts. Mary oversees all requests and interviews applicants herself. She has only two stipulations: recipients must be year-round residents, and Mary must pay the bills herself, helping recipients avoid the temptation of what she calls "the Poor People's Pub."

In deciding which requests to grant, Mary says, "I work with my heart instead of my head." Running her fund in this way over the years, she has helped 30 percent of Block Islanders pay medical, rent, mortgage, utility, and tuition bills; waterproof their basements after hurricanes; and buy ferry tickets to travel to the mainland for therapy—to name only a few in a long list of pressing needs. In some cases, Mary pays for financial counseling so applicants can learn to manage their money better.

When Mary talks about the needs of her neighbors, she says that taking the time to listen to them is one of the biggest gifts she can give—or that any of us can give. When applauded for her tireless work over many decades, Mary echoes the sentiments of the other generosity heroes in this book: "I am an ordinary person who has been gifted with this."

A young woman who grew up on Block Island and has known Mary (or, as she calls her, "Mary Mom") all her life sums up the heart and soul of Mary's unique gifts: "The most amazing thing I have learned from her is that helping your community, helping a neighbor, caring for a fellow human, is just what you do."

If I can stop one heart from breaking,

I shall not live in vain;

If I can ease one life the aching,

Or cool one pain,

Or help one fainting robin

Unto his nest again,

I shall not live in vain.

EMILY DICKINSON

"That's what I consider true generosity.

You give your all, and yet you always feel as if it costs

you nothing."

SIMONE DE BEAUVOIR

When Jesus said, "You shall love your neighbor as yourself," an expert in the law asked him, "And who is my neighbor?" Jesus replied: "A man was going down from Jerusalem to Jericho, and he fell among the robbers, who stripped him and beat him, and departed, leaving him half dead. Now by chance a priest was going down the road; and when he saw him, he passed by on the other side. So likewise a Levite, when he came to the place and saw him, passed by on the other side. But a Samaritan, as he journeyed, came to where he was; and when he saw him, he had compassion. He went to him and bound up his wounds, pouring on oil and wine.

Then he put the man on his own donkey, took him to an inn, and took care of him. The next day he took out two denarii and gave them to the innkeeper, saying, 'Take care of him; whatever you spend, I will repay you when I come back.' Which of these three, do you think, proved neighbor to the man who fell into the hands of robbers?" The expert in the law replied, "The one who showed mercy on him." And Jesus said to him, "Go and do likewise."

LUKE 10:27-37

IT IS MORE BLESSED TO GIVE THAN TO RECEIVE.

ACTS 20:35

*For George Eliot, generosity does not lie in the grand gesture
but in the ordinary moments of daily life.*

COUNT THAT DAY LOST

If you sit down at set of sun
And count the acts that you have done,
And, counting, find
One self-denying deed, one word
That eased the heart of him who heard,
One glance most kind
That fell like sunshine where it went—
Then you may count that day well spent.

But if, through all the livelong day,
You've cheered no heart, by yea or nay—
If, through it all
You've nothing done that you can trace
That brought the sunshine to one face—
No act most small
That helped some soul and nothing cost—
Then count that day as worse than lost.

GEORGE ELIOT

ACT AS IF WHAT YOU DO
MAKES A DIFFERENCE.
IT DOES. WILLIAM JAMES

REAL GENEROSITY
TOWARD THE FUTURE LIES IN
GIVING ALL
TO THE PRESENT.

ALBERT CAMUS

THE HABIT OF GIVING
ONLY ENHANCES THE
DESIRE TO GIVE.

WALT WHITMAN

> "I'VE LEARNED THAT YOU SHOULDN'T
> GO THROUGH LIFE WITH A CATCHER'S MITT
> ON BOTH HANDS. YOU NEED TO BE ABLE
> TO THROW SOMETHING BACK."
>
> MAYA ANGELOU

The Story of Betty Londergan

AFTER A SUCCESSFUL CAREER in advertising, this author of two books on parenting faced a crossroads in her life in 2008–9. She lost her job, watched her investments dramatically dwindle in the economic meltdown—and she became an "empty nester." Around the same time, she inherited $75,000 from her father. But receiving the money didn't answer the big question that she was struggling with: "What am I going to do with the rest of my life?"

The next chapter was not unfolding effortlessly.

And then Betty went to the movies. She saw *Julie and Julia*, based on Julie Powell's blog, in which she chronicled her culinary adventures as she cooked her way through

Julia Child's famous *The Art of French Cooking*, one recipe each day. As Betty stood in her kitchen the morning after seeing the movie, she rolled over and over in her head a new question: How she could be of service, in a way that would allow her to inspire a wide audience?

Betty intuitively sensed the power in a life of increased generosity. Looking back at that time, she reflects, "I was literally sick—so angry and frustrated. The only way I was going to get over it was to give my money away." In that moment, she decided to take half her inheritance, donate $100 each day for a year to a nonprofit organization, and then blog about the organization and the impact of the gift.

With $100 a day—$36,500 by the end of the year—and one post each day, Betty created what the *Huffington Post* was later to call "365 Love Letters to the World." She also created a legacy to her father's memory. To prepare, Betty made a list of 100 organizations that were making a difference in the world and that had personal meaning for her. She prepared her first 30 blog posts before the project's opening bell on January 1, 2010. After it launched, the project quickly took on a life of its own. Betty asked her readers to write to her about their favorite cause, project, or person, and then she set to work researching the responses. Her exuberant nature and offbeat sense of humor opened up connections and conversations with organizations of all sizes and missions. When Betty became convinced that a reader's cause was a worthy one, she made her donation and wrote about it for the blog. Looking back, she says, "I think I've used two of the posts I'd [originally] written and never referred to the list even once. People found me."

Betty was experiencing firsthand just how contagious generosity can be.

"I just don't see how it's possible to have so much and not feel compelled to give to those who are in such desperate need," Betty says. "If you have a roof over your head, you're one in a hundred in the world." While naysayers might ask what possible difference her gifts of only $100 could make, Betty stayed true to her commonsense philosophy of giving: "I think if you set out to change the world, you'll probably burn out in a week or two, but if you try to do a little bit of good in any way you can, you'll be the ripple in the water that just may spread out across your world. If something moves me, then I follow my heart."

The subject of considerable media attention, "365 Days of Putting My Money Where My Mouth Is," as Betty called her blog, became enormously popular, attracting a large and loyal audience. In many ways, Betty's voice was the counterpoint to the press coverage showered on powerful billionaire philanthropists. Her motto might have been Nike's "Just do it!" And, like all the generosity heroes of this book, Betty did not think she was doing anything remotely virtuous or noteworthy. In fact, she felt like the recipient of the gift, not the donor: "I'm lucky, lucky, lucky. Am I paying it forward? No. I'm paying it backward. I've been given so much. This is exactly what I should be doing."

The power of generosity ultimately freed Betty from her concerns about her own financial situation. "Giving away money is the absolute antidote to fear and insecurity about money," she says. "Desire and clutching cause suffering, and when you let go, it is a beautiful thing." As she made her daily gifts, Betty let go into an experience far more powerful than she had ever imagined it would be. As with many of those featured in this book, her experience demonstrated that we can actually strengthen our generosity muscle with repetitive practice and an open heart.

A life of service met a life of blogging as Betty embarked on her next project, traveling the world for Heifer International and writing intimate portraits of the people and communities at the heart of the organization's mission to end poverty and hunger, and care for the earth.

"To give away money is an easy matter

and in any man's power. But to decide to whom to give it,

and how large, and when, and for what purpose and how,

is neither in any man's power nor an easy matter."

ARISTOTLE

GIVING IS THE HIGHEST EXPRESSION OF POTENCY. ERICH FROMM

A. R. Ammons offers a poem on the generosity
of simply being.

THE CITY LIMITS

When you consider the radiance, that it does not withhold
itself but pours its abundance without selection into every
nook and cranny not overhung or hidden; when you consider

that birds' bones make no awful noise against the light but
lie low in the light as in a high testimony; when you consider
the radiance, that it will look into the guiltiest

swervings of the weaving heart and bear itself upon them,
not flinching into disguise or darkening; when you consider
the abundance of such resource as illuminates the glow-blue

bodies and gold-skeined wings of flies swarming the dumped
guts of a natural slaughter or the coil of shit and in no
way winces from its storms of generosity; when you consider

that air or vacuum, snow or shale, squid or wolf, rose or lichen,
each is accepted into as much light as it will take, then
the heart moves roomier, the man stands and looks about, the

leaf does not increase itself above the grass, and the dark
work of the deepest cells is of a tune with May bushes
and fear lit by the breadth of such calmly turns to praise.

A. R. AMMONS

"Winter comes to every one of us

sooner or later. And every spring, just like clockwork,

the garden is reborn. By the time we die the real

question is, 'What have we done to leave our garden

better prepared for spring—someone else's spring?'"

GEORGE VAILLANT

"I am of the opinion that my life belongs

to the whole community and as I live it is my privilege—

my privilege to do for it whatever I can. I want to be thoroughly

used up when I die, for the harder I work the more I love.

I rejoice in life for its own sake. Life is no brief candle to me;

it is a sort of splendid torch which I've got a hold of for the

moment and I want to make it burn as brightly as possible

before handing it on to future generations."

GEORGE BERNARD SHAW

ALTRUISM

What if we got outside ourselves and there
really was an outside out there, not just
our insides turned inside out? What if there
really were a you beyond me, not just
the waves off my own fire, like those waves off
the backyard grill you can see the next yard through,
though not well—just enough to know that off
to the right belongs to someone else, not you.
What if, when we said I love you, there were
a you to love as there is a yard beyond
to walk past the grill and get to? To endure
the endless walk through the self, knowing through a bond
that has no basis (for ourselves are all we know)
is altruism: not giving, but coming to know
someone is there through the wavy vision
of the self's heat, love become a decision.

MOLLY PEACOCK

MONEY IS LIKE MANURE;

IT'S NOT WORTH A THING

UNLESS IT'S SPREAD AROUND

ENCOURAGING YOUNG THINGS

TO GROW.

THORNTON WILDER

CHARITY SHOULD BEGIN AT HOME, BUT SHOULD NOT STAY THERE.

PHILLIPS BROOKS

IT IS MORE DIFFICULT TO GIVE MONEY AWAY INTELLIGENTLY THAN TO EARN IT IN THE FIRST PLACE.

ANDREW CARNEGIE

"Every man according as he purposeth

in his heart, so let him give; not grudgingly, or of necessity:

for God loveth a cheerful giver."

2 CORINTHIANS 9:7

"ONE WOULD GIVE GENEROUS ALMS IF YOU HAD THE EYES
TO SEE THE BEAUTY OF A CUPPED RECEIVING HAND."

GOETHE

The Story of Narayanan Krishnan

THE PRODUCT OF a middle-class upbringing and an elite college education, Narayanan Krishnan was an award-winning chef for India's famous Taj Hotels. In 2003, after having been awarded a prime post at a hotel in Switzerland, he decided to first return home to Madurai, India, to say goodbye to his family. As he was leaving one of the city's best hotels, he saw a homeless man on the side of the road, so devastated by hunger that he was eating his own human waste. Narayanan returned to the hotel and bought food for the starving man.

Narayanan had not been a stranger to the human suffering that surrounded him in his daily life in India. Yet as he watched the man devour the food he had brought him and saw his eyes fill with tears of gratitude, he heard an inner voice telling him to quit his new job and commit himself to feeding and tending to the hungry, destitute, ill, and forsaken of Madurai. Despite the objections of his family and friends, Narayanan had discovered his life's path.

Merging his newfound passion with his professional skills, he quickly formed a volunteer workforce that cooks and delivers three hot meals each day to more than 400 people in the city, those in the most serious need. He and his team rise at 4 a.m. to cook and take three 35-mile trips each day to deliver the food. Quite often, Narayanan will sit with the neediest and feed them by hand. Today his organization, Akshaya Trust, has delivered well over 1.2 million meals. What began with a moment is now a movement.

As Narayanan grew to know the people who counted on him for survival, he also saw the extent of the need for basic hygiene and care. He approached local barbers to ask for volunteers to give haircuts and shaves, but the barbers all refused to help the members of India's lowest caste, the ones historically regarded as "untouchable." So Narayanan took classes at a local salon and now always travels with his comb, razor, shaving brush, and soap. To date, he estimates that he has done about four thousand haircuts.

Narayanan's current project is the Akshaya Trust, whose centerpiece is Akshaya House, a complex of dorms, dining facilities, a clinic, and an acute-care facility. Located on 2.7 acres just outside of Madurai, the complex, with facilities for 100 men and women, is nearing completion.

Narayanan is often asked where he finds the energy for this work. His answer is always the same: "I get energy from them. The happiness I see on their faces keeps me going. I want to save my people. This is the purpose of my life."

The Sanskrit word *akshaya* means never-ending. And with 42 percent of the Indian population living below the international poverty line, according to World Bank estimates, Narayanan's work is truly never-ending. But so is his commitment. "The food gives them the physical nutrition, love and affection the mental nutrition," he says. "The ultimate purpose of life is to give. Start giving and you will feel the joy of giving."

And it all started with a moment.

TO GENEROUS SOULS EVERY TASK IS NOBLE. EURIPIDES

YOU HAVE NOT LIVED

UNTIL YOU HAVE DONE SOMETHING

FOR SOMEONE WHO CAN

NEVER REPAY YOU.

JOHN BUNYAN

"Past the seeker as he prayed came the

crippled and the beggar and the beaten. And seeing them . . .

he cried, 'Great God, how is it that a loving creator can

see such things and yet do nothing about them?'

God said, 'I did do something. I made you.'"

AUTHOR UNKNOWN

"Sometime in your life, hope that you might

see one starved man, the look on his face when the bread finally

arrives. Hope that you might have baked it or bought or even

kneaded it yourself. For that look on his face, for your meeting

his eyes across a piece of bread, you might be willing to lose

a lot, or suffer a lot, or die a little, even."

DANIEL BERRIGAN

"We who lived in concentration camps

can remember those who walked through the huts comforting

others, giving away their last piece of bread. They may have

been few in number, but they offer sufficient proof that

everything can be taken from a person but one thing:

the last of human freedoms—to choose one's attitude to

any given set of circumstances—to choose one's own way."

VIKTOR FRANKL

"For I was hungry, and you gave me something to eat; I was thirsty, and you gave me something to drink; I was a stranger, and you invited me in; naked, and you clothed me; I was sick, and you visited me; I was in prison, and you came to me. Then the righteous will answer him, 'Lord, when did we see you hungry and feed you, or thirsty and give you something to drink? And when did we see you a stranger and invite you in, or naked and clothe you? When did we see you sick, or in prison, and come to you?' The King will answer and say to them, 'Truly I say to you, to the extent that you did it to one of these brothers of mine, even the least of them, you did it to me.'"

MATTHEW 25:35

In this poem, Vachel Lindsay offers his wish for
a more generous world as the divine right of us all.

A NET TO SNARE THE MOONLIGHT

[What the Man of Faith said:]

The dew, the rain and moonlight
All prove our Father's mind.
The dew, the rain and moonlight
Descend to bless mankind.

Come, let us see that all men
Have land to catch the rain,
Have grass to snare the spheres of dew,
And fields spread for the grain.

Yea, we would give to each poor man
Ripe wheat and poppies red,
A peaceful place at evening
With the stars just overhead:

A net to snare the moonlight,
A sod spread to the sun,
A place of toil by daytime,
Of dreams when toil is done.

VACHEL LINDSAY

THE GROUND'S GENEROSITY
TAKES IN OUR COMPOST
AND GROWS BEAUTY!
TRY TO BE MORE
LIKE THE GROUND. RUMI

"If a poor man unknown to anyone comes

forth and says, 'I am hungry; give me something to eat,'

he should not be examined as to whether he might be an

imposter—he should be fed immediately."

MAIMONIDES

DO NOT REFUSE YOUR CHARITY EVEN TO THOSE WHO HAVE NO MERIT BUT THEIR MISERY.

LORD CHESTERFIELD

*As George Meredith points out, generosity can take the form
either of an obligation or of a high calling in our lives.*

THE BURDEN OF STRENGTH

If that thou hast the gift of strength, then know

Thy part is to uplift the trodden low;

Else in a giant's grasp until the end

A hopeless wrestler shall thy soul contend.

GEORGE MEREDITH

> "WHEN YOU LET GO OF TRYING TO GET MORE OF
> WHAT YOU DON'T REALLY NEED, IT FREES UP OCEANS
> OF ENERGY TO MAKE A DIFFERENCE WITH WHAT
> YOU HAVE. . . . WHEN YOU MAKE A DIFFERENCE
> WITH WHAT YOU HAVE, IT EXPANDS."
>
> LYNNE TWIST

The Story of the Salwen Family

SOMETIMES the lightning bolt of generosity strikes an entire family. In the case of the Salwens, it was 14-year-old Hannah who was inspired first. One day in 2006, in their hometown of Atlanta, Georgia, Hannah was sitting in traffic with her father, Kevin Salwen, an entrepreneur and *Wall Street Journal* reporter and editor. As they waited for the light to change, Hannah noticed that on one side of the car was a homeless beggar and on the other side was a man driving a black Mercedes convertible. Hannah speculated on just how much the homeless man and others like him could be helped if the Mercedes owner were to sell his car, buy a more modest one, and put some of the balance toward helping those in need: "Dad, if *that* man had a less nice car, *that* man there could have a meal." The light changed, but Hannah didn't let go of the moment.

"What do you want to do—sell our house?" Hannah's mother, Joan, finally asked as the family continued to discuss the incident in the days that followed. It wasn't a serious question, but she'd asked it and the words were out. The family began to speculate as to what it would be like if they were to dramatically alter their lives, shifting their focus from the classic American dream of accumulating material wealth to fulfilling another kind of dream. After weeks of family discussions, they decided to take the radical steps of selling their 6,500-square-foot home, moving to a modest home half its size and half its price, and donating half the proceeds from the sale ($800,000) to charity.

After researching nonprofit organizations that were doing work they particularly admired, the Salwens decided to sponsor health, microfinancing, food, and other programs for 30,000 villagers in more than 30 rural villages in Ghana, through the New York City–based development organization Hunger Project. In the moving book *The Power of Half: One Family's Decision to Stop Taking and Start Giving Back*, Kevin and Hannah document the family's journey, which took them halfway around the world and transformed their way of life. Kevin writes in the book's introduction, "This book is more than just the tale of a family trying to turn the good life into a life of good. It's about unintended consequences, like the way inventors stumbled across penicillin or Post-it notes or Flubber. Yes, we're helping the world a bit. But in the process we are transforming our relationships with one another. And that has been the real surprise."

Less welcome surprises were the negative reactions they received. They lost some friends. Others were skeptical about their motives and the extent of the impact they could really have. "I could never do that," people frequently told them. Says Kevin: "Who expects you to? Our project was never about size. We chose to sell our house because it was something that our family could handle from the perspective of giving half. But 'half' can be whatever you choose, at whatever budget you set." He found that there was a real value in setting that arbitrary standard: "Often when caring individuals see social problems, our gut reaction is 'I ought to do more.' But 'more' is too vague to be useful, and we usually end up not doing much of anything. By contrast, 'half' provides a metric to live with, a way to set a standard to push us to achieve."

One of the themes of their book is urging the reader to discover what his or her half can be—for example, half as much time in front of the television, half as many birthday or Christmas gifts, half a salary, half one's clothes. Hannah says, "Everyone has too much of something, whether it's time, talent, or treasure. Everyone does have their own half—you just have to find it."

"Setting out to be selfless became the most self-interested thing we ever did," Kevin says. "And it took a 14-year-old girl to kick us to this point." Upon hearing about the project, Archbishop Desmond Tutu praised Hannah and her family for their work, remarking, "We often say that young people must not let themselves be infected by the cynicism of their elders. Hannah inoculated her family with the vision to dream a different world, and the courage to help create it."

DON'T SAYTHAT YOU
WANT T<u>O</u> GIVE,
BUT GO AHEAD
AND GIVE!
YOU'LL NEVER CATCH UP
WITH A MERE HOPE. GOETHE

GO THE EXTRA MILE.
IT'S NEVER CROWDED.

AUTHOR UNKNOWN

"Riches, power, and fame last only for a few

years! Why do people cling so desperately to these transitory things?

Why can't people who have more than they need for themselves give

that surplus to their fellow citizens? Why should some people have

such a hard time during their few years on this earth?"

ANNE FRANK

THE MÉTIER OF BLOSSOMING

Fully occupied with growing—that's

the amaryllis. Growing especially

at night: it would take

only a bit more patience than I've got

to sit keeping watch with it till daylight;

the naked eye could register every hour's

increase in height. Like a child against a barn door,

proudly topping each year's achievement,

steadily up

goes each green stem, smooth, matte,

traces of reddish purple at the base, and almost

imperceptible vertical ridges

running the length of them:

Two robust stems from each bulb,

sometimes with sturdy leaves for company,

elegant sweeps of blade with rounded points.
Aloft, the gravid buds, shiny with fullness.
One morning—and so soon!—the first flower

has opened when you wake. Or you catch it poised
in a single, brief
moment of hesitation.
Next day, another,
shy at first like a foal,
even a third, a fourth,
carried triumphantly at the summit
of those strong columns, and each
a Juno, calm in brilliance,
a maiden giantess in modest splendor.
If humans could be
that intensely whole, undistracted, unhurried,
swift from sheer
unswerving impetus! If we could blossom
out of ourselves, giving
nothing imperfect, withholding nothing!

DENISE LEVERTOV

"While you have a thing it can be taken from you but when you give it, you have given it. No robber can take it from you. It is yours then forever when you have given it. It will be yours always. That is to give."

JAMES JOYCE

GENEROSITY ALLIES ITSELF
WITH AN INNER FEELING OF
ABUNDANCE
—THE FEELING THAT WE HAVE
ENOUGH TO
SHARE.

SHARON SALZBERG

"If every man took only what was sufficient

for his needs, leaving the rest to those in want, there would

be no rich and no poor."

ST. BASIL OF CAESAREA

THINGS OF THE SPIRIT

DIFFER FROM THINGS MATERIAL

— IN THAT —

THE MORE YOU GIVE

THE MORE YOU HAVE.

CHRISTOPHER MORLEY

As Shakespeare reminds us, even when we are completely absorbed
in romantic love, generosity often emerges to further enhance the glow.

My bounty is as boundless as the sea,

My love as deep; the more I give to thee,

The more I have, for both are infinite.

Romeo and Juliet

> ## "THE WINDS OF GRACE BLOW ALL THE TIME.
> ## ALL WE NEED TO DO IS SET OUR SAILS."
>
> SRI RAMAKRISHNA PARAMAHAMSA

The Story of Smitty Pignatelli

SMITTY PIGNATELLI, the state representative from my home district in Berkshire County, Massachusetts, has taught me more about true public service than anyone I know. I wish it were not so rare these days to encounter a person in elected office (one who must run for that office every two years!) who is so completely dedicated to helping people. Not remotely interested in power, wealth, or the trappings of a distinguished career, Smitty serves the people of his region literally each and every day. And then he looks for more ways to serve.

As the events following Hurricane Katrina unfolded, Smitty, like most of us, was heartbroken as he watched helplessly. And, like many of us, he found it hard to know how to help. But his big heart and his intuition moved him in remarkable directions.

Sixteen months after Katrina, Smitty volunteered to spend Christmas week of 2006 in New Orleans, working on a project to build bicycles. Quite by chance, a resident of the Ninth Ward, whose family had been especially hard hit during the hurricane, stopped by one afternoon to lend a hand. Moved by Stanley Stewart's powerful and unique presence, Smitty asked around to find out more about this man. After getting directions to Stanley's house, Smitty dropped by for a visit with the Stewart family of six, in their small FEMA trailer that had gotten electricity only the month before. Stanley gave Smitty a tour of what was left of his house. It was on the top floor of this house that Stanley and 11 members of his family had huddled together waiting to be rescued after 14 feet of water had destroyed all their possessions and nearly taken their lives.

Smitty was seized by the desire to do what he could, and spent the following week stripping walls and tearing out most traces of the devastation. As he prepared to pack up and head home, Stanley asked the helpers to form a prayer circle of gratitude and told his new friend from Massachusetts, "If you ever need anything, you can count on me."

Stanley, who had nothing left to give, was offering everything.

At that moment, Smitty says, he felt something akin to "divine intervention." He knew he had to keep moving forward in this work that had been mysteriously put in his path for a reason. He returned four months later with a team of roofers to put a new roof on the house. After that job was completed and Smitty was driving away, he looked back to see Stanley standing on the front stoop, blowing kisses. Once again, Smitty realized, "I'm not done yet."

Over the nine months between his Christmas visit and late September 2007, Smitty made nine trips to New Orleans in his commitment to help rebuild the house and life of the Stewart family. Once he went down for just one day to double-check that his measurements of the kitchen were correct. During that time, he raised $30,000 locally and received $150,000 in donated materials from friends in Berkshire County. In September, joined by 25 friends and friends of friends, Smitty headed to the Stewart house, where they spent the equivalent of $90,000 in donated skilled labor over the course of six long days to completely reconstruct the dwelling: new structural framing; electrical, plumbing, heating, and air-conditioning systems; doors; windows; hardwood floors; kitchen cabinets; bathroom fixtures; sheetrock and paint. To fulfill a long-held dream of one of the Stewart daughters, Smitty even brought along hot-pink paint for her bedroom.

The Stewart family was beyond grateful. Their lives and home had been rebuilt by a team of 25 strangers while many just like them, or even worse off, still lived in impossible circumstances. But the real gift for Smitty was that 25 people's lives "were changed forever by assisting one family 1,500 miles away." Years later, the reactions of the men who participated in this project offer moving testimony to the power of generosity. One man suddenly retired, vowing to "keep life in perspective." Another, who returned with a new relationship to his work and family, now says, as only a sentimental tough guy can, "You wrecked me!" A third said the New Orleans week was "the greatest thing I've ever done in my life."

It goes without saying that Smitty sees no special virtue in what he did. None of the heroes in this book do. As he summed it up for me in one of our many conversations about this pivotal chapter in his life: "I think it's inside every one of us. A fire had to be lit."

For Smitty, it all started with a moment of curiosity and compassion. *Who is this man? What does he need? How have he and his family made it through this unimaginable time? How can I help?* In many ways, it is a simple story of a moment of recognition and the path of generosity that unfolded from that moment. But, as Smitty recognizes, those moments are all around us.

We need only open our eyes and hearts to them.

DO ALL THE GOOD YOU CAN,

BY ALL THE MEANS YOU CAN,

IN ALL THE WAYS YOU CAN,

IN ALL THE PLACES YOU CAN,

AT ALL THE TIMES YOU CAN,

TO ALL THE PEOPLE YOU CAN,

AS LONG AS EVER YOU CAN.

JOHN WESLEY

"There is a wonderful mythical law of nature

that the three things we crave most in life—happiness, freedom,

and peace of mind—are always attained by giving them to

someone else."

PEYTON CONWAY MARCH

THE ONLY GIFT IS A PORTION OF THYSELF.

RALPH WALDO EMERSON

"If there is anything I have learned about

men and women, it is that there is a deeper spirit of altruism

than is ever evident. Just as the rivers we see are minor

compared to the underground streams, so, too, the idealism

that is visible is minor compared to what people carry in

their hearts unreleased or scarcely released."

ALBERT SCHWEITZER

CHARITY

Whate'er thou wouldst receive at others' hands,
Thou first to them must freely give away;
Whether of houses high or spreading lands,
Nought shall be thine till thou hast seen this day;
God gives thee all; but canst thou all receive,
When e'en my little thou dost yet refuse?
No longer then thy brother's spirit grieve,
And thou shalt have yet larger gifts to use;
For in my Father's house do many live,
Who, older far, in love have stronger grown,
And how to them can'st thou e'er learn to give,
Who all the Father hath can call their own?
Give freely then, for all thou giv'st away
Shall men with added gifts to thee repay.

JONES VERY

IF YOU THINK YOU ARE TOO SMALL

TO BE **EFFECTIVE,**

YOU HAVE NEVER BEEN IN BED

WITH A MOSQUITO.

BETTY REESE

Lord, make me an instrument of your peace.

Where there is hatred, let me sow love;

Where there is injury, pardon;

Where there is doubt, faith;

Where there is despair, hope;

Where there is darkness, light;

And where there is sadness, joy.

O Divine Master, grant that I may not so much seek

to be consoled as to console;

to be understood as to understand;

to be loved as to love.

For it is in giving that we receive;

it is in pardoning that we are pardoned;

and it is in dying that we are born to eternal life.

PRAYER OF SAINT FRANCIS OF ASSISI

GENEROSITY GIVES ASSISTANCE RATHER THAN ADVICE.

MARQUIS DE VAUVENARGUES

The Story of Cami Walker

IN HER EARLY thirties and newly married, Cami Walker was working as an advertising executive when she was suddenly struck down by severe and debilitating multiple sclerosis. The disease quickly took away the use of her hands and the vision in one eye, and left her with numbness throughout her body.

Among the many healers she called upon during this crisis was an African medicine woman named Mbali Creasso. The prescription Cami received from Mbali, in what she called a "divination," has its roots in a Dagara African ritual. The directions were clear and relatively simple: "Give away 29 gifts in 29 days." Mbali's reasoning was equally straightforward: "Healing doesn't happen in a vacuum, but through our interactions with other people. By giving, you are focusing on what you have to offer others, inviting more abundance into your life. Giving of any kind is taking a positive action that begins the process of change. It will shift your energy for life." Further, the gifts Cami was to give had to be both authentic and mindful—and one needed to be something that she felt was scarce in her life.

At first skeptical of such a nontraditional healing agenda, but committed to doing all she could to regain her health, Cami quickly became amazed at the transformation that giving made in her life. Her daily gifts were simple—a Kleenex, a kind word, a phone call, a seashell. By the end of the month, her health had dramatically improved, and she attributes this to a profound shift in her mindset that provided her with freedom and joy as she set about healing.

As with the other generosity heroes in these pages, Cami realized early in her giving project that the gifts were only the vehicles through which her generous spirit could manifest. "We're not here to live in a vacuum," she reflects. "We're here to be of service to each other and have a common experience."

When Mbali looks back on her own first experience with this giving ritual, she remarks on its relevance to our lives in the Western world today. "Though most of us have no experience of the depth of scarcity that exists in African countries, we often believe we are not successful enough, rich enough, beautiful or thin enough. We simply don't have enough or are not good enough. We become so lost in our sense of lack, low self-esteem, and nonexistent self-love that we forget that our life is an essential part of a greater whole, and that we have many gifts to offer to the world at large."

Throughout her journey back to health, Cami kept a journal, which eventually became her inspirational book *29 Gifts: How a Month of Giving Can Change Your Life*. It's a day-by-day account of her month of giving, the people she met, the insights that she experienced, and the renewal of her health. She has continued her own monthly giving every day since her encounter with her transformational healer, and her experience of healing through giving inspired her to earn a graduate degree in integrative medicine. She went on to establish a Transformative Education curriculum at a noted hospital and now works in the integrative bodywork program there.

WE MAKE A LIVING BY WHAT WE GET, BUT WE MAKE A LIFE BY WHAT WE GIVE.

WINSTON CHURCHILL

NO ONE HAS EVER BECOME POOR BY GIVING. ANNE FRANK

In this poem, Czeslaw Milosz reminds us that sometimes
it is our sense of gratitude and wonder, our appreciation of beauty
and abundance, that opens the door to our innate generosity.

GIFT

A day so happy.

Fog lifted early. I worked in the garden.

Hummingbirds were stopping over the honeysuckle flowers.

There was no thing on earth I wanted to possess.

I knew no one worth my envying him.

Whatever evil I had suffered, I forgot.

To think that once I was the same man did not embarrass me.

In my body I felt no pain.

When straightening up, I saw the blue sea and sails.

CZESLAW MILOSZ

"Happiness exists on earth, and it is won

through prudent exercise of reason, knowledge of the harmony

of the universe, and constant practice of generosity."

JOSÉ MARTÍ

YOU WILL DISCOVER THAT YOU HAVE

TWO HANDS.

ONE IS FOR HELPING YOURSELF

AND THE OTHER IS FOR

HELPING OTHERS.

AUDREY HEPBURN

"Giving opens the clenched fist

of self-contraction into the open hand of generosity.

We release self—a prime engine of suffering—

when we give from the heart."

RICK HANSON

For many, generosity requires immediate action,
not only for its own benefit but also to spare us from later regret.

CAST YOUR BREAD

Cast your bread for it's good to give
and he whose hand is open will thrive—
lest, in the end, the days deceive you
and strip you of all you've denied.

SHMUEL HANAGID

"When you become detached mentally

from yourself and concentrate on helping other people

with their difficulties, you will be able to cope with your

own more effectively. Somehow, the act of self-giving

is a personal power-releasing factor."

NORMAN VINCENT PEALE

"Nirvana manifests as ease, as love,

as connectedness, as generosity, as clarity, as unshakeable

freedom. This isn't watering down nirvana. This is the

reality of liberation that we can experience, sometimes

in a moment and sometimes in transformative ways

that change our entire life."

JACK KORNFIELD

THE WILLINGNESS TO SHARE DOES NOT MAKE ONE CHARITABLE; IT MAKES ONE FREE.

ROBERT BRAULT

"Generous behavior shines a protective light over the entire life span. Generous behavior is closely associated with reduced risk of illness and mortality and lower rates of depression. Even more remarkable, giving is linked to traits that undergird a successful life, such as social competence, empathy, and positive emotion. By learning to give, you become more effective at living itself."

STEPHEN POST

> "NO ONE CAN MEASURE THE EFFECTS OF A SINGLE
> ACT OF GIVING, FOR ITS REPERCUSSIONS ARE
> BEYOND OUR LIMITED IMAGINATION."
>
> TAITETSU UNNO

The Story of Samuel Stone

DURING THE CHRISTMAS season of 1933, at the height of the Great Depression, Samuel J. Stone of Canton, Ohio, secretly gave away 150 gifts of $5 each to neighbors who were suffering from hunger, cold, illness, and all manner of deprivation and pain. Mr. Stone was so careful to protect his identity, and that of the recipients of his generosity, that only the most unusual circumstances brought his story to light 75 years later. The only generosity hero featured in this book who is no longer living, Mr. Stone was one of the great anonymous donors. His story and identity came into the spotlight in 2008 through his grandson's book, *A Secret Gift*—a poignant reminder of the power of one person's generosity for many generations and immeasurable lives.

A Romanian-born Jew, Sam Stone fled a life of persecution in 1902 for the promise of the American Dream. He eventually settled in Canton, where he married, raised a family, and established a successful chain of clothing stores. While always grateful for all that his American life had brought him, Sam was not known for any particular acts of generosity. But in 2008, many years after his death, one of his three daughters decided to give a suitcase of family memorabilia to her son Ted. A noted investigative reporter and head of the journalism department at Emerson College in Boston, Ted Gup soon realized that the contents of this suitcase provided a dramatic window on an unknown chapter in his grandfather's life. The suitcase contained hundreds of letters and cancelled checks that, after months of tracking down, revealed his grandfather's remarkable secret gift.

On December 17, 1933, a man who called himself B. Virdot placed an ad in the *Canton Repository* newspaper, offering help to his fellow citizens in the most extreme need during the holiday season. Promising that he would never reveal their identity, he asked only that they write him a letter describing their financial circumstances and what they would do with the gift of $5 (the equivalent of $100 today) that he was offering. The contents of the suitcase that Ted Gup opened revealed the 150 letters that Sam Stone received as B. Virdot, and the cancelled checks signed B. Virdot that he had mailed in response.

We have all heard stories of the agonies of the Great Depression. But to read through these letters as presented in Gup's book is to gain a new understanding of what life was like at a time of staggering unemployment, savings devastated in bank failures, famine, disease, and no social services as we know them today. Orphanages and prisons were overflowing. People scavenged for coal along the railroad tracks. Pillars of the community lost their homes, businesses, all their savings. Hundreds of people in Canton were in dire straits.

The collective spirit of the time is also poignantly revealed in each letter. Most letters asked for help for others—many said they would rather starve than ask for help for themselves. Others said that Mr. Virdot's ad had given them courage to go on. It was a time of neighbor helping neighbor—doctors, grocery stores, milk companies donating their goods and services with little chance of ever being paid. Against this backdrop, a Romanian Jew who had immigrated to this country to escape persecution experienced his own lightning bolt of generosity in his desire to give back—during their holiest season—to the largely Christian community in which he had settled and thrived. His gift was doubly generous for its anonymity (see Maimonides, page 104).

That Sam Stone's story speaks to us so forcefully today is a testament to the resonance that remarkable generosity has in our lives. Ted Gup's *New York Times* Op Ed account of his grandfather's secret generosity is the second most e-mailed article in *Times* history. The vibrant memories of the children and grandchildren of the recipients of Sam Stone's gifts, which make up the core of Gup's book, dramatically demonstrate just how much difference one person's seemingly modest acts of generosity can make—sometimes all the difference.

CENTRAL TO JUDAISM IS THE CONCEPT OF *TZEDAKAH* (charity, justice, fairness, righteousness). The twelfth-century Jewish philosopher Maimonides organized tzedakah into eight steps, which he called the Ladder of Charity.

THE FIRST DEGREE OF GIVING:

To give to the poor but grudgingly.

THE SECOND DEGREE OF GIVING:

To give with good grace, but not enough.

THE THIRD DEGREE OF GIVING:

To give, but only after being asked.

THE FOURTH DEGREE OF GIVING:

To give before (or without) being asked.

THE FIFTH DEGREE OF GIVING:

To give without knowing the identity of who
will benefit from the gift.

THE SIXTH DEGREE OF GIVING:

To give without the beneficiary of the gift knowing
the donor's identity.

THE SEVENTH DEGREE OF GIVING:

To give without either party knowing the other's identity.

THE EIGHTH DEGREE OF GIVING:

To fight poverty by enabling the poor to escape from their
poverty.

NOBODY MADE A GREATER MISTAKE
THAN HE WHO DID NOTHING
BECAUSE HE COULD ONLY DO
A LITTLE. EDMUND BURKE

BREAD FOR MYSELF
IS A MATERIAL QUESTION.
BREAD FOR MY NEIGHBOR
IS A SPIRITUAL ONE.

NICHOLAS BERDYAEV

O MAY I JOIN THE CHOIR INVISIBLE

[Excerpt]

O may I join the choir invisible

Of those immortal dead who live again

In minds made better by their presence; live

In pulses stirred to generosity,

In deeds of daring rectitude, in scorn

For miserable aims that end with self,

In thoughts sublime that pierce the night like stars,

And with their mild persistence urge man's search

To vaster issues.

So to live is heaven:

To make undying music in the world . . .

GEORGE ELIOT

ONE MUST BE POOR TO KNOW THE LUXURY OF GIVING!

GEORGE ELIOT

"When you are harvesting in your field and you overlook a sheaf, do not go back to get it. Leave it for the alien, the fatherless, and the widow, so that the Lord your God may bless you in all the work of your hands. When you beat the olives from your trees, do not go over the branches a second time. Leave what remains for the alien, the fatherless, and the widow. When you harvest the grapes in your vineyard, do not go over the vines again. Leave what remains for the alien, the fatherless, and the widow. Remember that you were slaves in Egypt. That is why I command you to do this."

DEUTERONOMY 24:19-22

THERE IS NO BETTER EXERCISE
FOR YOUR HEART
THAN REACHING DOWN
AND HELPING TO
LIFT SOMEONE UP.

BERNARD MELTZER

*We are often struck by the seemingly small generosities of
the past whose impact threads its way through our lives.*

THOSE WINTER SUNDAYS

Sundays too my father got up early
and put his clothes on in the blueblack cold,
then with cracked hands that ached
from labor in the weekday weather made
banked fires blaze. No one ever thanked him.

I'd wake and hear the cold splintering, breaking.
When the rooms were warm, he'd call,
and slowly I would rise and dress,
fearing the chronic angers of that house,

Speaking indifferently to him,
who had driven out the cold
and polished my good shoes as well.
What did I know, what did I know
of love's austere and lonely offices?

ROBERT HAYDEN

"At times our own light goes out

and is rekindled by a spark from another person.

Each of us has cause to think with deep gratitude

of those who have lighted the flame within us."

ALBERT SCHWEITZER

"O you who believe!

Do not cancel your charity,

by giving reminders of your generosity,

or by injury, like those who spend

their wealth to be seen by men,

but believe neither in God nor in the Last Day."

THE KORAN 2:264

> "THE TRUE MEASURE OF A MAN IS HOW HE TREATS
> SOMEONE WHO CAN DO HIM ABSOLUTELY NO GOOD."
>
> SAMUEL JOHNSON

The Story of Paul Wagner

PAUL WAGNER had never thought of himself as an unusually generous person. He'd done his fair share of good deeds—adopted four rescue pets; run the United Way drive at his office, where he was a purchasing agent; and organized various local food drives in his hometown of Philadelphia. But he had never been drawn to make any sort of grand gesture of generosity—until the day before Thanksgiving 2005. On that particular day, Paul was reading the *New York Times*, as was his habit, and happened upon an article about a new nonprofit, MatchingDonors.com, that pairs living donors with individuals in urgent need of an organ transplant.

Paul knew little about this area of need but was moved by the statistics. Nearly 100,000 Americans are awaiting an organ donation at any given time, and each has about a 50/50 chance of receiving one. The average wait for a donation is seven to nine years, and eight thousand people (more than 20 each day) die while waiting. In 2009, there were 28,000 transplant surgeries. Until recently, most organ donations had been from cadavers and were managed through UNOS, the United Network for Organ Sharing. But MatchingDonors.com offered a new vehicle for connecting donors with people who came forward to make their requests public.

Paul was staggered by the enormity and urgency of the need. On the website, he read the stories of those hoping for donations and found himself particularly drawn to the story of Gail Tomas, a 65-year-old former opera singer, music teacher, and mother of two who wrote on the site, "I desperately need your help to live." Gail needed a kidney donation. Reading her story, Paul was struck by a lightning-bolt awareness of the power of his own generosity and immediately made the decision to donate. Despite the objections of his partner, family, and friends, he moved forward with the process. On Valentine's Day 2006, Paul donated his left kidney to Gail and saved her life.

Much controversy surrounds the issue of organ donation, particularly the issue of donors being able to choose among recipients on sites like MatchingDonors.com. Most of the original skeptics now admit that the founders of the site, entrepreneur Paul Dooley and Dr. Jeremiah Lowney, have opened promising new avenues for patients who otherwise would have no choice but to wait on the long and typically very slow-moving UNOS list. As testament to the spirit of generosity that this organization has tapped, Dooley and Lowney say they have over 6,800 "angels" who have signed up to donate an organ to 400 potential recipients on the site. MatchingDonors.com now receives well over a million and a half hits per month.

Paul describes his decision to donate his kidney to Gail as easy and natural. "It has been one of the best decisions I have ever made," he says. "Who couldn't (respond to) that story? This was a real human being who had a family, and whose family wanted to keep their mother. And I just couldn't turn my back on that." Paul always knew that he wanted to be able to look back on his life and say that he gave more than he took. "I just wanted to do something good. That's my payment. You can't buy that with money."

It's all I have to bring today—
This, and my heart beside—
This, and my heart, and all the fields—
And all the meadows wide—
Be sure you count—should I forget
Some one the sum could tell—
This, and my heart, and all the Bees
Which in the Clover dwell.

EMILY DICKINSON

"Everybody can be great. Because anybody

can serve. You don't have to have a college degree to serve.

You don't have to make your subject and your verb agree to serve.

You don't have to know the second theory of thermodynamics

in physics to serve. You only need a heart full of grace.

A soul generated by love."

DR. MARTIN LUTHER KING JR.

"Believe, when you are most unhappy,

that there is something for you to do in the world. So long as you

can sweeten another's pain, life is not in vain."

HELEN KELLER

"By practicing true generosity you can come

to see that there is no separation between the one who gives

and the one who receives. In giving, one receives; and in receiving,

one also gives."

FRANK JUDE BOCCIO

WHAT I WOULD GIVE

What I would like to give them for a change
is not the usual prescription with
its hubris of the power to restore,
to cure; what I would like to give them, ill
from not enough of laying in the sun
not caring what the onlookers might think
while feeding some banana to their dogs—
what I would like to offer them is this,
not reassurance that their lungs sound fine,
or that the mole they've noticed change is not
a melanoma, but instead of fear
transfigured by some doctorly advice
I'd like to give them my astonishment
at sudden rainfall like the whole world weeping,

and how ridiculously gently it

slicked down my hair; I'd like to give them that,

the joy I felt while staring in your eyes

as you learned epidemiology

(the science of disease in populations),

the night around our bed like timelessness,

like comfort, like what I would give to them.

RAFAEL CAMPO

FIND OUT HOW MUCH
GOD HAS GIVEN YOU
AND FROM IT TAKE WHAT
YOU NEED;
THE REMAINDER IS NEEDED
BY OTHERS.

SAINT AUGUSTINE

"When someone gives you something precious,

it means that, beyond the usefulness of the gift, you are precious.

The gift marks a moment when you are welcomed into the other

person's heart."

JOHN TARRANT

"In a profoundly interdependent world,

generosity is fundamental to the entire economy of life. Even the

simplest biological function involves receiving something from

others (nutrients, oxygen, life), processing it in some unique way,

and then passing it on to all other members of the matrix of life.

We all do this whether we want to or not, and whether or not

we are aware of it. The practice of giving becomes perfected

when we align ourselves very deeply with this truth,

by consciously and mindfully offering everything we do or say—

even everything we think—as an act of universal generosity."

ANDREW OLENDZKI

"It is one of the most beautiful compensations

of this life that no man can sincerely try to help another without

helping himself."

RALPH WALDO EMERSON

"I expect to pass through life but once.

If, therefore, there be any kindness I can show, or any good

thing I can do to any fellow being, let me do it now, and not

defer or neglect it, as I shall not pass this way again."

WILLIAM PENN

"THERE IS NO BEAUTIFIER OF COMPLEXION, OR FORM, or behavior, like the wish to scatter joy and not pain around us. 'Tis good to give a stranger a meal, or a night's lodging. 'Tis better to be hospitable to his good meaning and thought, and give courage to a companion. We must be as courteous to a man as we are to a picture, which we are willing to give the advantage of a good light."

RALPH WALDO EMERSON

The Story of Petra Nemcova

As she prepared for a vacation in Thailand with her fiancé in December 2004, Petra Nemcova felt as if she were living a charmed life. A successful high-fashion model, she had recently become engaged to "the love of her life," British photographer Simon Atlee. Taking a break from their non-stop schedules, Petra and Simon decided to spend a few weeks in late December on the beaches of Khao Lak.

Midway into their time there, on December 26, Khao Lak was struck by the earthquake and tsunami that killed 283,000 people and left millions homeless in 11 countries. In a flash, the world that Petra knew was gone. While trying to reach safe ground, Simon was swept away by the wave. Petra was washed to the top of a palm tree, where she clung to the branches for eight hours until help arrived. Airlifted inland to a hospital, she was found to have suffered multiple breaks in her pelvis and serious internal injuries. "I was so broken I couldn't move," she recalls.

After long hospitalizations in Thailand and Czechoslovakia, and with great determination, Petra recovered over the following months and vowed to devote her energies to helping other victims of natural disasters. In 2005, she returned to Thailand to find out how she could help most effectively. There she saw firsthand the tragedies that remain after emergency relief runs out: families without homes, orphaned children, and entire communities decimated. On this visit, she experienced the particularly poignant devastation during what is called "the gap period"—after first-response teams leave and before governments are able to step in. This experience gave her the impetus to start an organization that would specifically address this vast unmet need.

Happy Hearts Fund, the nonprofit foundation that Petra formed, is dedicated to rebuilding schools and restoring hope and opportunity in the lives of children after natural disasters. The foundation goes to work after emergency response has ended, implementing sustainable practices to ensure lasting impact. HHF is now active in nine countries and has built or rebuilt 56 schools and kindergartens. Since its founding, it has benefited more than 34,000 children and 337,000 members of impacted communities.

Many generous people throughout the world put their energy and resources into starting nonprofits that make a difference. But there are special lessons for all of us when one individual who had no particular relationship to philanthropy is suddenly jolted into extraordinarily generous giving and doing what she can. It doesn't take a tsunami. We all have friends, neighbors, and colleagues who have experienced tragedy and emerged from it dedicated to helping others in similar straits. The extent of Petra's impact in her dedication to this work is a beacon to the naysayers who insist that one person can't change the world.

Says Petra: "Every experience has pluses and minuses. If we focus on the minuses, we go down the spiral. But if we are able to focus on the pluses, we can become stronger and put more meaning into our life. We have a choice. Sometimes it seems very hard, but the best way to heal physically or emotionally is to keep positive."

Generosity is such a choice.

THE PROPER AIM

OF GIVING

IS TO PUT THE RECIPIENTS

IN A STATE WHERE

THEY NO LONGER

NEED OUR GIFTS.

C. S. LEWIS

KINDNESS IN WORDS
CREATES CONFIDENCE.

KINDNESS IN THINKING
CREATES PROFOUNDNESS.

KINDNESS IN GIVING
CREATES LOVE. LAO TZU

We all have gifts to share. For poets like Jimmy Santiago Baca,
the greatest generosity may be in the words they offer.

I AM OFFERING THIS POEM

I am offering this poem to you,
since I have nothing else to give.
Keep it like a warm coat
when winter comes to cover you,
or like a pair of thick socks
the cold cannot bite through,

I love you,

I have nothing else to give you,
so it is a pot full of yellow corn
to warm your belly in winter,
it is a scarf for your head, to wear
over your hair, to tie up around your face,

I love you,

Keep it, treasure this as you would
if you were lost, needing direction,
in the wilderness life becomes when mature;
and in the corner of your drawer,
tucked away like a cabin or hogan
in dense trees, come knocking,
and I will answer, give you directions,
and let you warm yourself by this fire,
rest by this fire, and make you feel safe

I love you,

It's all I have to give,
and all anyone needs to live,
and to go on living inside,
when the world outside
no longer cares if you live or die;
remember,

I love you.

JIMMY SANTIAGO BACA

NOT BEING ABLE TO DO EVERYTHING IS NO EXCUSE FOR NOT DOING EVERYTHING YOU CAN.

ASHLEIGH BRILLIANT

THE TEST OF OUR PROGRESS
IS NOT WHETHER WE ADD MORE
TO THE ABUNDANCE OF
THOSE WHO HAVE MUCH;
IT IS WHETHER WE PROVIDE
ENOUGH FOR THOSE
WHO HAVE TOO LITTLE.

FRANKLIN D. ROOSEVELT

KINDNESS

Before you know what kindness really is
you must lose things,
feel the future dissolve in a moment
like salt in a weakened broth.
What you held in your hand,
what you counted and carefully saved,
all this must go so you know
how desolate the landscape can be
between the regions of kindness.
How you ride and ride
thinking the bus will never stop,
the passengers eating maize and chicken
will stare out the window forever.

Before you learn the tender gravity of kindness,
you must travel where the Indian in a white poncho

lies dead by the side of the road.
You must see how this could be you,
how he too was someone
who journeyed through the night with plans
and the simple breath that kept him alive.

Before you know kindness as the deepest thing inside,
you must know sorrow as the other deepest thing.
You must wake up with sorrow.
You must speak to it till your voice
catches the thread of all sorrows
and you see the size of the cloth.

Then it is only kindness that makes sense anymore,
only kindness that ties your shoes
and sends you out into the day to mail letters and purchase bread,
only kindness that raises its head
from the crowd of the world to say
it is I you have been looking for,
and then goes with you everywhere
like a shadow or a friend.

NAOMI SHIHAB NYE

"Like humility, generosity comes from seeing that everything we have and everything we accomplish comes from God's grace and God's love for us. In the African understanding of *ubuntu*, our humility and generosity also come from realizing that we could not be alive, nor could we accomplish anything, without the support, love, and generosity of all the people who have helped us to become the people we are today. Certainly it is from experiencing this generosity of God and the generosity of those in our life that we learn gratitude and to be generous to others." ARCHBISHOP DESMOND TUTU

" 'What is not given is lost.'

These words were spoken by Father Ceyrac,

a French Jesuit missionary who has devoted

himself to the well-being of children in South

India for over 60 years. A similar thought is found

in Buddhist teaching: 'What is not done for the

benefit of others is not worth doing.

Seeking happiness just for yourself is the best way

there is to make yourself, and everyone else, unhappy.' "

MATTHIEU RICARD

THE FRAGRANCE ALWAYS REMAINS
IN THE HAND
THAT GIVES THE ROSE.

HEDA BEJAR

> "NEVER WORRY ABOUT NUMBERS. HELP ONE
> PERSON AT A TIME, AND ALWAYS START WITH
> THE PERSON NEAREST YOU."
>
> MOTHER TERESA

The Story of Reed Sandridge

WE ALL KNOW that life's most challenging chapters can call forth the very best in human nature. As millions coped with a dramatically changed world and painful personal circumstances during the economic catastrophe of 2008–9, some of those most deeply affected found ways to bring the practice of generosity to the forefront of their lives.

When Reed Sandridge was laid off from his job at a Washington DC nonprofit in October 2009, becoming unemployed for the first time in his life, he was struck—swiftly, surprisingly, and with utter clarity—by the inspiration to transform his misfortune by giving what he could to others. Two months later, in honor of his late mother—who taught him that difficult economic times make it even more important to share with others—Reed embarked on what he called his Year of Giving. Each day for the next year, he walked through Washington and gave $10 to a complete stranger.

The reactions he received ran the gamut. Many people turned him down, suspicious of what might be expected in return. Others rejected his offer because they felt "unworthy." Reed tried to engage in conversation all those who accepted his offer, asking them what they would use the money for and what meaning it held for them. Those in serious need told him they would use it to buy a meal; some headed off to Starbucks with their unexpected gift; others were eager to pass it on to someone in greater need. But, invariably, those who took the $10 realized that it was not about the money—they were on the receiving end of a spontaneous act of generosity.

As he ran into these recipients over the next year, he heard over and over that the gifts were "less about the small giveaways than about spreading the idea of doing small kindnesses," he says. The small gesture of a seemingly insignificant giveaway put Reed in touch with what it feels like to give from one's heart and, as he looked into the eyes of his recipients, what it feels like to accept generosity from a stranger. Day after day, Reed was able to strengthen and flex his "generosity muscle." During the 365 days, he kept a blog collecting the often remarkable stories of the lives he touched.

The end of the year brought Reed into a new relationship with giving as he created a program that supported other unemployed individuals to become "Kindness Investors" for seven days and continue the $10-a-day giving tradition. Now employed as a regional director for a leading conservation organization, Reed has also embarked on a Year of Volunteering, during which he has committed to volunteer at least once a week, and to work with companies and organizations to create corporate volunteer programs. Reed is also the executive director of the Urban Philharmonic, a small nonprofit that brings orchestral music to diverse areas of Washington.

ATTENTION IS THE RAREST AND PUREST FORM OF GENEROSITY.

SIMONE WEIL

GIVE WHAT YOU HAVE.

TO SOMEONE, IT MAY BE BETTER THAN

YOU DARE TO THINK.

HENRY WADSWORTH LONGFELLOW

"Practice giving things away, not just things

you don't care about, but things you do like. Remember,

it is not the size of the gift, it is its quality and the amount

of mental attachment you overcome that count. So don't

bankrupt yourself on a momentary positive impulse,

only to regret it later. Give thought to giving. Give small things,

carefully, and observe the mental processes going along

with the act of releasing the little thing you liked."

ROBERT THURMAN

Generosity does not always have the appearance that we expect.
As James Wright shows us in this poem, it is a wonderful habit to be on
the lookout for where generosity might pop up, completely unsuspected.

HOOK

I was only a young man
In those days. On that evening
The cold was so God damned
Bitter there was nothing.
Nothing. I was in trouble
With a woman, and there was nothing
There but me and dead snow.
I stood on the street corner
In Minneapolis, lashed
This way and that.
Wind rose from some pit,
Hunting me.
Another bus to Saint Paul
Would arrive in three hours,

If I was lucky.
Then the young Sioux
Loomed beside me, his scars
Were just my age.
Ain't got no bus here
A long time, he said.
You got enough money
To get home on?
What did they do
To your hand? I answered.
He raised up his hook into the terrible starlight
And slashed the wind.
Oh, that? he said.
I had a bad time with a woman. Here,

You take this.
Did you ever feel a man hold
Sixty-five cents
In a hook,
And place it
Gently
In your freezing hand?

I took it.
It wasn't the money I needed.
But I took it.

JAMES WRIGHT

IN THIS WORLD, MONKS,
THERE ARE THREE THINGS
OF VALUE FOR ONE WHO GIVES.

WHAT ARE THESE THINGS?

BEFORE GIVING, THE MIND
OF THE GIVER IS HAPPY.

WHILE GIVING, THE MIND OF
THE GIVER IS MADE PEACEFUL.

AND HAVING GIVEN, THE MIND
OF THE GIVER IS UPLIFTED.

THE BUDDHA,
ANGUTTARA NIKAYA 3.6.37

"Once I was young, poor, and generous.

Now I have a house and a car and savings account, and I am not so generous. Gratitude, the simple and profound feeling of being thankful, is the foundation of all generosity. I am generous when I believe that right now, right here, in this form and this place, I am myself being given what I need. Generosity requires that we relinquish something, and this is impossible if we are not glad for what we have. Otherwise the giving hand closes into a fist and won't let go."

SALLIE JIKO TISDALE

MINUTES

Minutes swarm by, holding their dirty hands out,
Begging change, loose coins of your spare attention.
No one has the currency for them always;
Most go unnoticed.

Some are selling packets of paper tissues,
Some sell thyme they found growing wild on hillsides,
Some will offer shreds of accordion music,
Sad and nostalgic.

Some have only cards with implausible stories,
Badly spelled in rickety, limping letters,
"Help me—deaf, etcetera—one of seven
Brothers and sisters."

Others still accost the conspicuous lovers,
Plying flowers looted from cemeteries,
Buds already wilting, though filched from Tuesday's
Sumptuous funeral.

Who's to say which one of them finally snags you,
One you will remember from all that pass you,
One that makes you fish through your cluttered pockets,
Costing you something:

Maybe it's the girl with the funeral roses,
Five more left, her last, and you buy the whole lot,
Watching her run skipping away, work over,
Into the darkness;

Maybe it's the boy with the flute he fashioned
Out of plastic straws, and his strident singing,
Snatches from a melody in a language
No one can teach you.

A. E. STALLINGS

IF YOU ARE NOT GENEROUS
WITH A MEAGER INCOME,
YOU WILL NEVER BE GENEROUS
WITH ABUNDANCE.

HAROLD NYE

> "YOU CAN MEASURE THE DEPTH OF PEOPLE'S
> AWAKENING BY HOW THEY SERVE OTHERS."
>
> KOBO DAISHI

The Story of Elissa Montanti

GRIEVING THE LOSS of her mother and grandmother, Elissa Montanti, a medical technician from Staten Island, decided to volunteer to help others going through difficult times. In 1996, there was considerable media coverage of the huge need for supplies for children in war-torn Bosnia. In a meeting that Elissa attended with Muhamed Sacirbey, the Bosnian Ambassador to the United Nations, she offered to do what she could to raise money for these supplies. In response, Sacirbey pulled from his desk a letter from a young Bosnian boy, Kenan Malkic, who had stepped on a land mine and lost two arms and a leg. Kenan's plea was for "God and all merciful people to help me getting prosthetics."

In that moment, Elissa says, her life changed. "I knew it right then and there, that second," she recalls. She immediately started recruiting airlines, hospitals, doctors, and prosthetic companies to donate their products and services. Before long, Kenan and his mother were staying at Elissa's home in Staten Island as he embarked on surgeries and treatments that gave him two new arms, a new leg, and a new life.

With little money, no political connections, and no training in philanthropic relief, Elissa founded the Global Medical Relief Fund (GMRF, www.gmrfchildren.org) to aid children who are missing limbs or eyes, have been severely burned, or have been injured due to war, natural disaster, or illness. Over the past 16 years, she has continued to create teams that make miracles happen for children all over the world.

Elissa's approach to fundraising is revolutionary. When approaching potential funders, she says, "I expect them to help. I'm grateful—but how could you not help?" Her passion and determination have paid off again and again. While it is still sometimes difficult to pay the light bill, she has made it possible for more than 100 children to come to the United States from Europe, Africa, the Middle East, and Asia for life-changing treatments, surgery, and prosthetic limb and eye fittings. Today, her closest partner in the ongoing work of GMRF is Kenan Malkic, the Bosnian boy, now grown, who wrote the letter that set Elissa on this path.

In spreading the word of her organization's global reach, Elissa believes that the most important voices are those of the children themselves. Each child becomes "an ambassador of what is best in America," she says.

And, I would add, each child becomes an ambassador for the power of generosity.

"When a candle is lit in a dark room, it illuminates the room to some extent, but its power is limited. But if you use the same candle to light another candle, the total brightness increases. If you continue to do this, you can fill the room with brilliant illumination. The idea of transferring merit to others is like this. If we keep our own light selfishly hidden, it will only provide a limited amount of illumination. But when we share our light with others, we do not diminish our own light. Rather, we increase the amount of light available to all. Therefore, when others light our candle, we issue forth light. When out of gratitude we use our candle to light other people's candles, the whole room gets brighter. This is why we transfer merit to others. This kind of light is continuous and inexhaustible." MASTER SHENG YEN

A PERSON'S TRUE WEALTH

IS THE GOOD

HE OR SHE DOES

IN THE WORLD. MOHAMMED

The grateful heart opens pathways to the generous heart,
as we hear in this hymn by John Greenleaf Whittier.

HYMN OF THE CHILDREN

Sung at the anniversary of the Children's Mission, Boston, 1878

Thine are all the gifts, O God!
   Thine the broken bread;
Let the naked feet be shod,
   And the starving fed.
Let Thy children, by Thy grace,
   Give as they abound,
Till the poor have breathing-space,
   And the lost are found.
Wiser than the miser's hoards
   Is the giver's choice;
Sweeter than the song of birds
   Is the thankful voice.

Welcome smiles on faces sad
   As the flowers of spring;
Let the tender hearts be glad
   With the joy they bring.
Happier for their pity's sake
   Make their sports and plays,
And from lips of childhood take
   Thy perfected praise!

JOHN GREENLEAF WHITTIER

THE BEST WAY TO FIND YOURSELF, IS TO LOSE YOURSELF IN THE SERVICE OF OTHERS. GANDHI

THE GREATEST GOOD

YOU CAN DO FOR ANOTHER

IS NOT JUST TO

SHARE YOUR RICHES

BUT TO REVEAL TO HIM

HIS OWN. BENJAMIN DISRAELI

"What is the use of living,

if it be not to strive for noble causes

and to make this muddled world

a better place for those who will live in it

after we are gone?"

WINSTON CHURCHILL

"The true meaning of life

is to plant trees under whose shade

you do not expect to sit."

NELSON HENDERSON

> "OF THOSE WHO HAVE BEEN GIVEN MORE,
> MORE WILL BE EXPECTED."
>
> MATTHEW 25:29

The Story of Leonard Abess

WHILE WE HAVE grown accustomed to news accounts of corporate philanthropy and impressive gifts made by the wealthiest among us, examples of true, personal generosity motivated by a profound sense of integrity among the country's one percent are all too rare. The story of Leonard Abess's generosity provides a stunning example of how wealthy businesspeople could ignite a profound shift in our society.

Leonard's father arrived in Miami in 1925 with $75. In 1946, he and a partner invested half a million dollars to form City National Bank of Florida. Over the years, Mr. Abess built a successful bank that he sold in the 1980s to an investor group, but which fell into bankruptcy soon after the purchase. In 1985, Leonard was able to buy back his father's bank for $21 million in borrowed money. Over the next 25 years, he brought new life to the bank, growing it from seven branches with $400 million in assets to 18 branches with $2.75 billion. Or, as Leonard would say, it was his employees who did all this.

Over the years, Leonard received many offers to buy the bank, and in 2008, Caja Madrid, the second largest bank in Spain, made him an offer he couldn't refuse. Under the terms of the agreement, all the employees' jobs would remain secure, Leonard would maintain an 83 percent interest and continue to run the bank, and the philosophy of generous giving to the community would be maintained. He sold the bank for $977 million.

What came next was no surprise to those who know Leonard Abess. He did not need to be struck by the lightning of generosity—generosity was already firmly implanted in his DNA. He says that what he did next he had been planning to do "for a very long time, probably more than 20 years."

What did he do? He took $60 million of his profits and divided it among all of the bank's 399 employees and 72 former employees—clerks, tellers, bookkeepers, secretaries, janitors, executives, everyone on the payroll. He had always felt that the bank's success depended on these employees: "I saw that if the president doesn't come to work, it's not a big deal. But if the teller doesn't show up, it's a serious problem. I knew some of these people since I was seven years old. I didn't feel right getting the money myself."

The day that the gifts were distributed Leonard stayed home, well out of the limelight. He didn't blog or tweet about what he'd done. He didn't hire a public-relations firm or alert the media. In fact, he declined all interviews except one with Diane Sawyer to tell the story for the record. The employees reported that as the envelopes containing their bonuses were passed out, one by one, there were no whoops or shouts. Says bank employee Carleatha Barbary, "We continued banking and tried to put an extra touch on what we were doing. Not that we don't do that all the time."

But the story got out, and President Obama invited Leonard Abess to attend his first address to Congress in January 2009, where he was seated next to the First Lady.

The person Leonard invited to accompany him was not a family member, corporate colleague, or dignitary. Instead, he brought a friend who had been with the bank for 51 years. She had been his boss in the print shop when he started out at the bank, and eventually became a safe-deposit custodian.

There will be skeptics who say that Leonard had so much money that his gifts to his employees were just a drop in the bucket. I urge you to consider what all the drops in all the buckets could add up to. As with all truly generous acts, the gift is far more than the money. As Leonard Abess said when asked about his decision to give, "I prefer to live in a world where this is ordinary."

NOBLESSE OBLIGE, OR, SUPERIOR ADVANTAGES BIND YOU TO LARGER GENEROSITY.

RALPH WALDO EMERSON

I WOULD RATHER HAVE IT SAID

"HE LIVED USEFULLY" THAN

"HE DIED RICH."

BENJAMIN FRANKLIN

"It has always seemed strange to me . . .

the things we admire in men, kindness and generosity, openness,

honesty, understanding, and feeling, are the concomitants of

failure in our system. And those traits we detest, sharpness, greed,

acquisitiveness, meanness, egotism, and self-interest, are the traits

of success. And while men admire the quality of the first they love

the produce of the second."

JOHN STEINBECK

*While our ability to give changes and evolves throughout our lives,
our generous spirit can always serve as a beacon to guide whatever
gifts we make, large or small.*

HIS ALMS

Here, here I live,

And somewhat give

Of what I have

To those who crave,

Little or much,

My alms is such;

But if my deal

Of oil and meal

Shall fuller grow,

More I'll bestow;

Meantime be it

E'en but a bit,

Or else a crumb,

The scrip hath some.

ROBERT HERRICK

THINK OF GIVING NOT AS A DUTY BUT AS A PRIVILEGE.

JOHN D. ROCKEFELLER

THE HIGHEST USE OF CAPITAL

IS NOT TO MAKE MORE MONEY

BUT TO MAKE MONEY DO MORE

FOR THE BETTERMENT OF LIFE.

HENRY FORD

SURPLUS WEALTH

— IS A —

SACRED TRUST

WHICH ITS POSSESSOR IS BOUND

TO ADMINISTER FOR THE GOOD

— OF THE —

COMMUNITY.

ANDREW CARNEGIE

"KEEP FEELING THE NEED FOR BEING FIRST.
BUT I WANT YOU TO BE THE FIRST IN LOVE.

I WANT YOU TO BE THE FIRST IN MORAL
EXCELLENCE. I WANT YOU TO BE THE
FIRST IN GENEROSITY."

DR. MARTIN LUTHER KING JR.

BENEVOLENCE

[Excerpt]

Now, thou mayst give
The famish'd food, the prisoner liberty,
Light to the darken'd mind, to the lost soul
A place in heaven. Take thou the privilege
With solemn gratitude. Speck as thou art
Upon earth's surface, gloriously exult
To be co-worker with the King of kings.

LYDIA HOWARD HUNTLEY SIGOURNEY

REGARD YOUR NEIGHBOR'S GAINS

AS YOUR OWN GAIN,

AND YOUR NEIGHBOR'S LOSS

AS YOUR OWN LOSS.

T'AI SHANG KAN YING P'IEN

"When we become more fully aware

that our success is due in large measure to the loyalty,

helpfulness, and encouragement we have received from

others, our desire grows to pass on similar gifts."

WILFERD A. PETERSON

"A generous heart is never lonesome.

A generous heart has luck. The lonesomeness

of contemporary life is partly due to the failure

of generosity."

JOHN O'DONOHUE

IT IS **NOT** THAT
SUCCESSFUL PEOPLE
ARE GIVERS;
IT IS THAT GIVERS ARE
SUCCESSFUL PEOPLE.

PATTI THOR

"IT IS A DENIAL OF JUSTICE NOT TO STRETCH OUT
A HELPING HAND TO THE FALLEN; THAT IS THE
COMMON RIGHT OF HUMANITY."

SENECA

The Story of Sal Dimisali

THE SON OF a beautician and a tool-and-die maker, Sal Dimisali grew up in extreme
poverty on Chicago's West Side. His father's gambling addiction kept the family
from having even the bare necessities of life. Never able to pay their bills and contin-
uously being evicted, they were constantly on the move. "We lived like gypsies," Sal
recalls. "I know how it feels to watch your mother cry when the electricity is turned off
and you have no food." At age 12, Sal got his first job. Even at that young age, he was
determined to live a life of service, to do everything he could to help those most in need.

Today, Sal is a successful 60-year-old real estate executive in Lake Geneva, Wisconsin,
and he has not forgotten that commitment. Early on, he donated to nonprofit organizations, but he didn't like the idea that a chunk of his hard-earned money was going
to their overhead. Instead, he decided to start his own nonprofit that would have no

overhead. In 1989, The Time Is Now to Help was born. Sal now helps about 500 people a year with food, rent, utilities, and other basic necessities. Over the years, this father of four has given away several million dollars to about 20,000 people—and shows no signs of stopping. His wife warns him that if he doesn't watch out, he will be in the same financial shape as those he supports. Sal responds, "I am just addicted to helping. It is contagious."

The organization receives 20 to 30 requests each week, and Sal and a group of volunteers verify each applicant's need, often going to the house and looking in their cabinets. "I do not want to give a hard-earned dollar to someone who is taking advantage," Sal says. "But once I verify that their need is genuine, my heart opens right up." He understands all too well the urgency of the requests. Often the first thing he makes possible is a hot meal for someone who is hungry, or a warm motel room for someone whose heat has been turned off. Then he tackles the bigger picture. "There is no bureaucratic red tape. I want to help people now," he says. But his help does not stop with money. Sal sits down and helps them make a budget, plan how they will be able to get back on their feet, find a job, or negotiate a lower rent. "It's not just a Band-Aid to feed them for that day. We get them back on a track so that their pride is given back to them. They can catch up."

In addition to supporting his own community of Lake Geneva, Sal is also committed to helping the small, deeply impoverished community of Pembroke Township in Hopkins Park, Illinois, 70 miles southwest of Chicago. Years ago, he was driving home from Chicago and noticed a collection of what appeared to be abandoned shacks. In fact, these falling-down dwellings, with dirt floors, no running water, and no electricity, were inhabited by people in the most desperate poverty. Sal took on their cause. He has renovated houses; bought trailers, food, and supplies; and arranged for the worst off to move to nearby apartments. A community that had been forgotten is now getting back on its feet, one person and one family at a time.

For several years, the Lake Geneva Regional News has run a popular weekly column written by an anonymous author. Now everybody knows who is writing what locals refer to as "Dear Abby for the down and out." Sal uses the column to focus on one person or family in the most dire straits, whose life has begun to turn around thanks to the gentle push of generosity. Where does he find the drive and determination to do what he does, day in and day out? Sal says, "I have a fire deep inside me."

"But history will judge you, and as the years pass,

you will ultimately judge yourself, in the extent to which you have

used your gifts and talents to lighten and enrich the lives of your fellow

men. In your hands lies the future of your world and the fulfillment

of the best qualities of your own spirit."

ROBERT F. KENNEDY

"Whatever a man has in superabundance

is owed, of natural right, to the poor for their sustenance.

So Ambrosias says, and it is also to be found in the Decretum

Gratiani: 'The bread which you withhold belongs to the hungry;

the clothing you shut away, to the naked; and the money you bury

in the earth is the redemption and freedom of the penniless.'"

ST. THOMAS AQUINAS

WITH GENTLENESS,
OVERCOME ANGER.

WITH GENEROSITY,
OVERCOME MEANNESS.

WITH TRUTH,
OVERCOME DELUSION.

BUDDHA, THE DHAMMAPADA

"Though I speak with the tongues of men
and of angels, and have not charity, I am become as a sounding
brass, or a tinkling cymbal.

And though I have the gift of prophecy,
and understand all mysteries, and all knowledge; and though
I have all faith, so that I could remove mountains, and have
not charity, I am nothing.

And though I bestow all my goods
to feed the poor, and though I give my body to be burned,
and have not charity, it profiteth me nothing."

ST. PAUL, I CORINTHIANS, 13:1–3

We never know who will be moved by our small acts of kindness, just as poets never know who will be moved by the generosity of their words.

POEM TO BE READ AT 3 A.M.

Excepting the diner
On the outskirts
The town of Ladora
At 3 a.m.
Was dark but
For my headlights
And up in
One second-story room
A single light
Where someone

Was sick or
Perhaps reading
As I drove past
At seventy
Not thinking
This poem
Is for whoever
Had the light on.

DONALD JUSTICE

THE WISE MAN
DOES NOT LAY UP
HIS OWN TREASURES.
THE MORE HE GIVES
TO OTHERS,
THE MORE HE HAS
FOR HIS OWN.

LAO TZU

DISCOVER WHAT BEING GENEROUS MEANS, AND BEGIN LIVING IT.

ST. AUGUSTINE

Acknowledgments

THIS BOOK IS a surprise. I have always been fascinated by stories of transformational generosity. In 2008, I found myself collecting these stories. As often happens when we focus our attention, the stories then started appearing from everywhere, pouring into my computer almost daily. At the same time, poems and quotations on generosity started finding their way to me. In 2011, I gave myself the time to immerse in the material and embark on more formal research. With the encouragement of friends and family, I realized the possibility of a little book of inspirations was beginning to take form. In early 2012, I took a winter sabbatical in order to focus exclusively on what that form might be. *Inspiring Generosity* is the result of that exploration.

As a first-time author, I had no experience in how such a book project might ever see the light of day. Through a beautiful coincidence, I connected with Josh Bartok at Wisdom Publications, who shared my enthusiasm for this book and took it on as masterful editor, guide, expert, and cheerleader. The book quite simply would not have happened without Josh, Laura Cunningham, Lydia Anderson, and the great team at Wisdom.

In many ways, this book's real authors are the 14 "generosity heroes" whose stories I tell here. Most have had some media coverage. Some have written books about their journeys to generosity. I bring them together in these pages to shine a new spotlight on their stories and the inspiration they offer.

An army of wonderful people in my life came together in support of the notion that, with utterly no experience in writing one, I had a book in me. First and foremost, my daily gratitude goes to my children, to whom the book is dedicated. Stephen Cope is a perpetual source of inspiration and encouragement in all things, now including the writing of books. Tresca Weinstein was my writing comrade and editor every step of the way, giving elegance and encouragement to my early scribblings. Heather Rose worked her design magic in crafting an early vision of the book. Mu Soeng and Andy Olendzki at the Barre Center for Buddhist Studies cheered me along, as did my wonderful friend and now fellow author Sharon Salzberg. Jim Gimian offered generous time, inspiration, encouragement, and advice. Millie Calesky taught me how to crack the whip in being a disciplined writer. Rabbi Debbie Zecher and the Reverend Natalie Shiras offered wonderfully thoughtful perspectives. Smitty Pignatelli shared his story and deeply personal reflections over many lunches together. Laurie Norton Moffatt and Mary Martin Niepold are special friends to this book and its author. Michelle Gillett, Stefanie Wortman, Rob Foreman, Zelda Austen, and my wonderful nephew and poet Stephen Cushman stepped forward to offer inspiring poems. My daughter, Alexandra Socarides, a Dickinson scholar, brought the two poems of that magnificent poet to me. My son-in-law, Gabriel Friend, offered invaluable practical advice. It took an exceedingly generous village that I am grateful to call home!

Permissions

The stories of the fourteen "generosity heroes" in this book were taken from accounts readily available in the media and in some cases amplified by correspondence and personal interviews. For a complete bibliography of sources that guided my work as well as suggested readings on generosity please go to the book's website: www.inspiring generosity.net.

Index of Names

About the Author

BARBARA BONNER started her professional life as an art historian, moving on to leadership positions at three New York City museums. She later served as Vice President of Bennington College and Kripalu Center for Yoga and Health. She now has her own consulting practice focused on helping nonprofits transform their philanthropic support. Committed to a life in philanthropy, she has served on 10 nonprofit boards and has started a fund to serve women with cancer in her region. She is currently board chair at the Barre Center for Buddhist Studies. A perpetual student of contemplative traditions and yoga as well as an avid gardener, she lives in a converted barn in the beautiful Berkshire hills of western Massachusetts. She is the inordinately proud mother of an actor and an English professor and grandmother of blessed Archer and Nate.

About Wisdom Publications

WISDOM PUBLICATIONS is the leading publisher of contemporary and classic Buddhist books and practical works on mindfulness. Publishing books from all major Buddhist traditions, Wisdom is a nonprofit charitable organization dedicated to cultivating Buddhist voices the world over, advancing critical scholarship, and preserving and sharing Buddhist literary culture.

To learn more about us or to explore our other books, please visit our website at www.wisdompubs.org. You can subscribe to our e-newsletter or request our print catalog online, or by writing to:

Wisdom Publications
199 Elm Street
Somerville, Massachusetts 02144 USA

You can also contact us at 617-776-7416, or info@wisdompubs.org.

Wisdom is a 501(c)(3) organization, and donations in support of our mission are tax deductible.

Wisdom Publications is affiliated with the Foundation for the Preservation of the Mahayana Tradition (FPMT).

Also from Wisdom Publications

Daily Doses of Wisdom
A Year of Buddhist Inspiration
Edited by Josh Bartok
448 pages | $16.95 | ebook $12.35

"Directions: Read one page a day. Side effects may include insight, compassion, and wisdom. Stop immediately if experiencing nirvana."
—Sumi Loundon, author of *Blue Jean Buddha*

The Clouds Should Know Me By Now
Buddhist Poet Monks of China
Edited by Red Pine and Mike O'Connor
224 pages | $15.95 | ebook $11.62

"Achingly beautiful poems."
—*Library Journal*

A Heart Full of Peace
Joseph Goldstein
128 pages | $9.95 | ebook $9.95

"Joseph Goldstein presents his thoughts on the practice of compassion, love, kindness, restraint, a skillful mind, and a peaceful heart as an antidote to the materialism of our age."
—*Spirituality & Practice*

One City
A Declaration of Interdependence
Ethan Nichtern
192 pages | $15.95 | ebook $11.62

"Resonant and refreshing."
—*The American Prospect*